DRAGONFLIES COLORING BOOK FOR KIDS!

DISCOVER THIS COLLECTION OF COLORING PAGES

Bold Illustrations
COLORING BOOKS

This is a Bleed Through Page If You Are Using a Colouring Marker or Pen!
Find Other Great Titles By searching for Bold Illustrations on Your Favorite Book Retailer
Amazon.Ca | Barnes & Noble (BN.Com) | Books A Million (BAM.Com)

Bold Illustrations
COLORING BOOKS

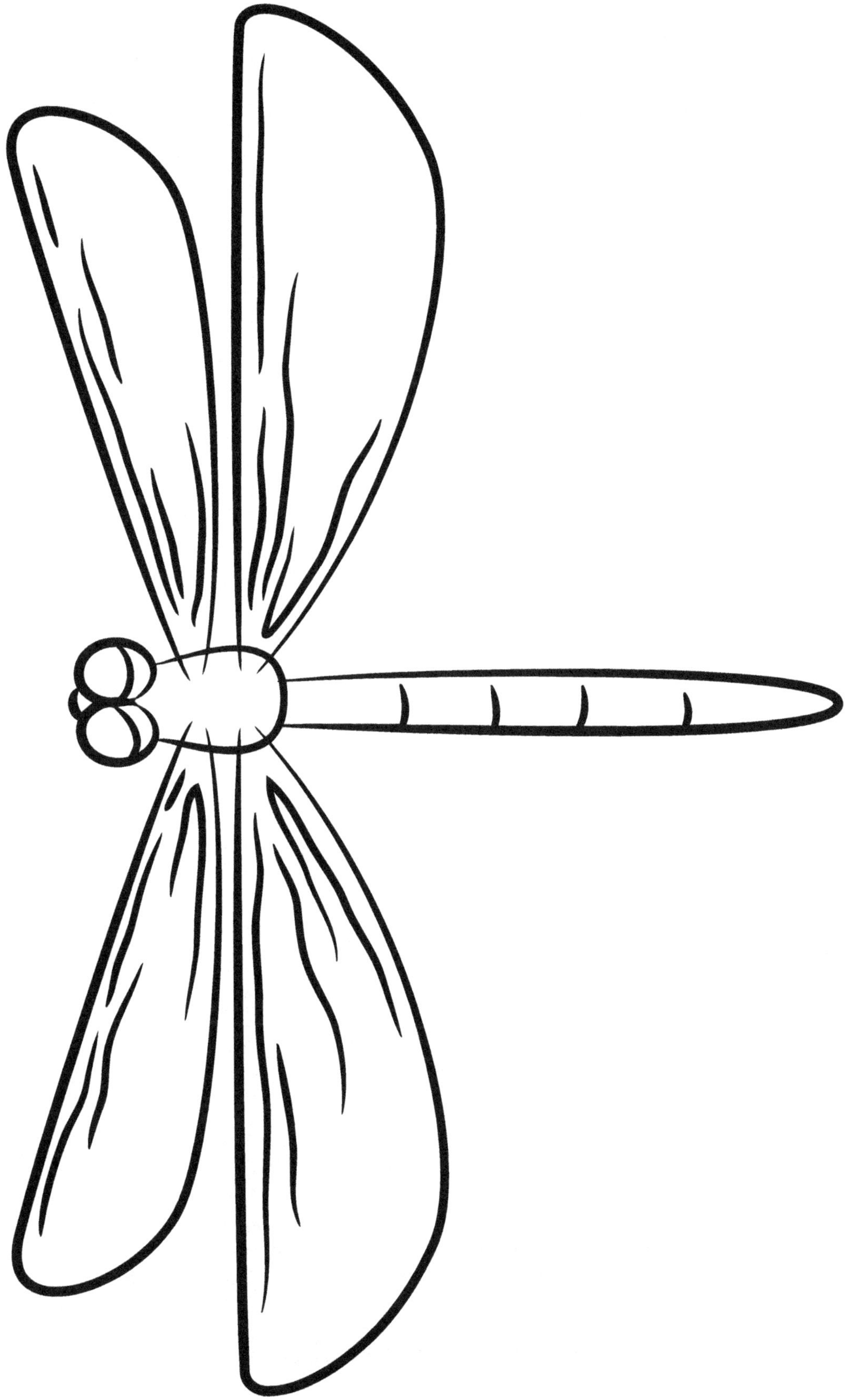

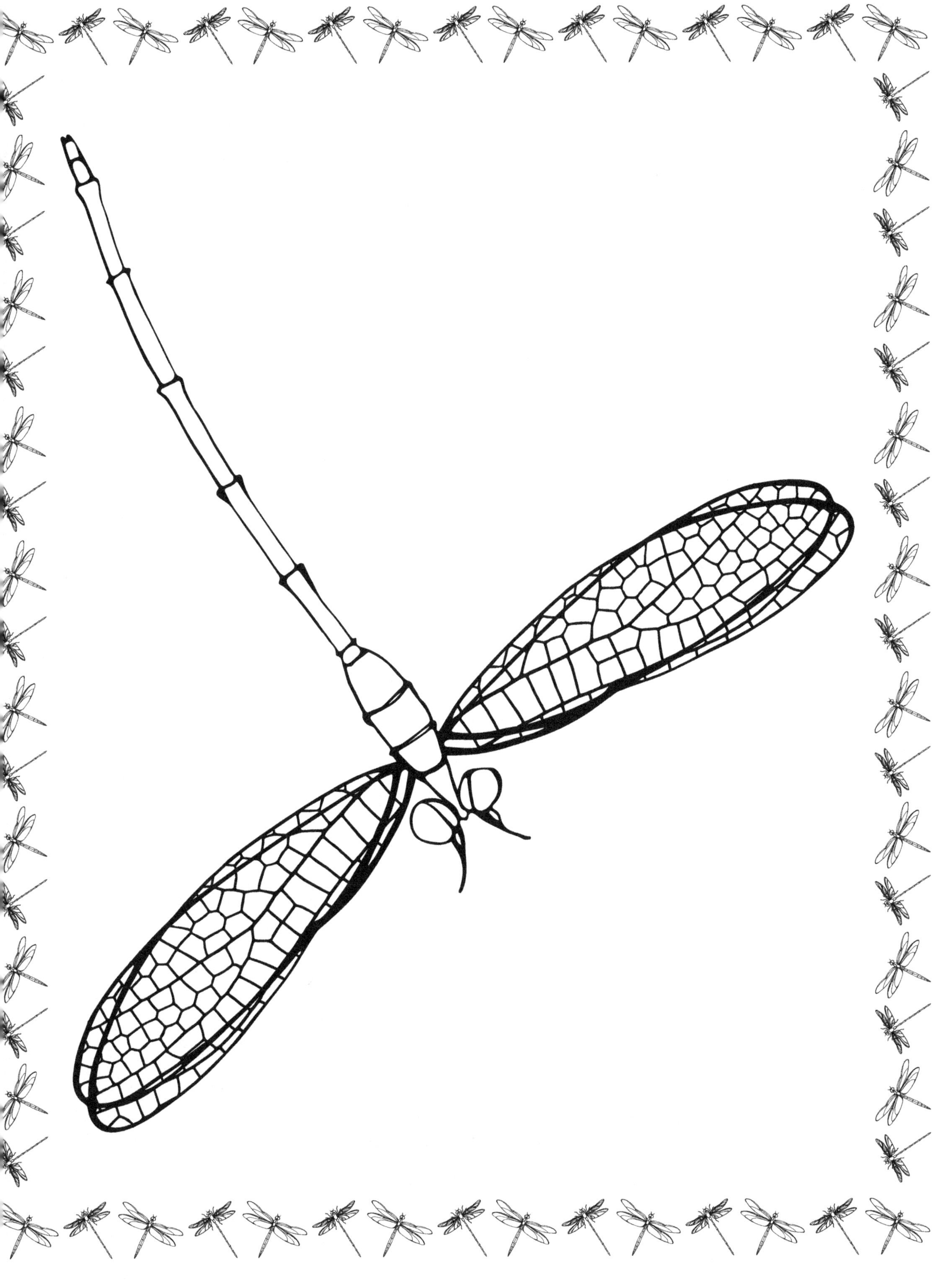

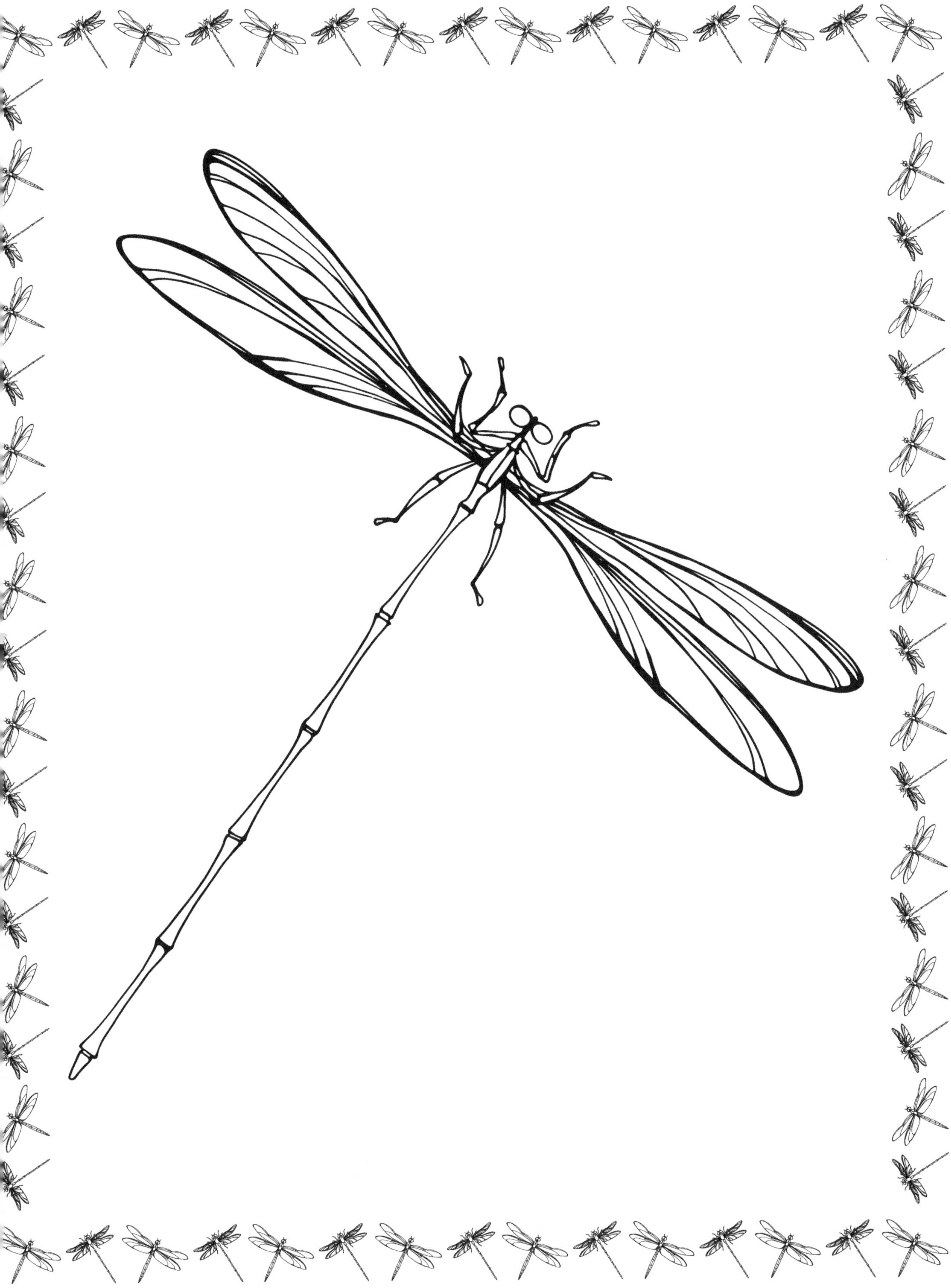

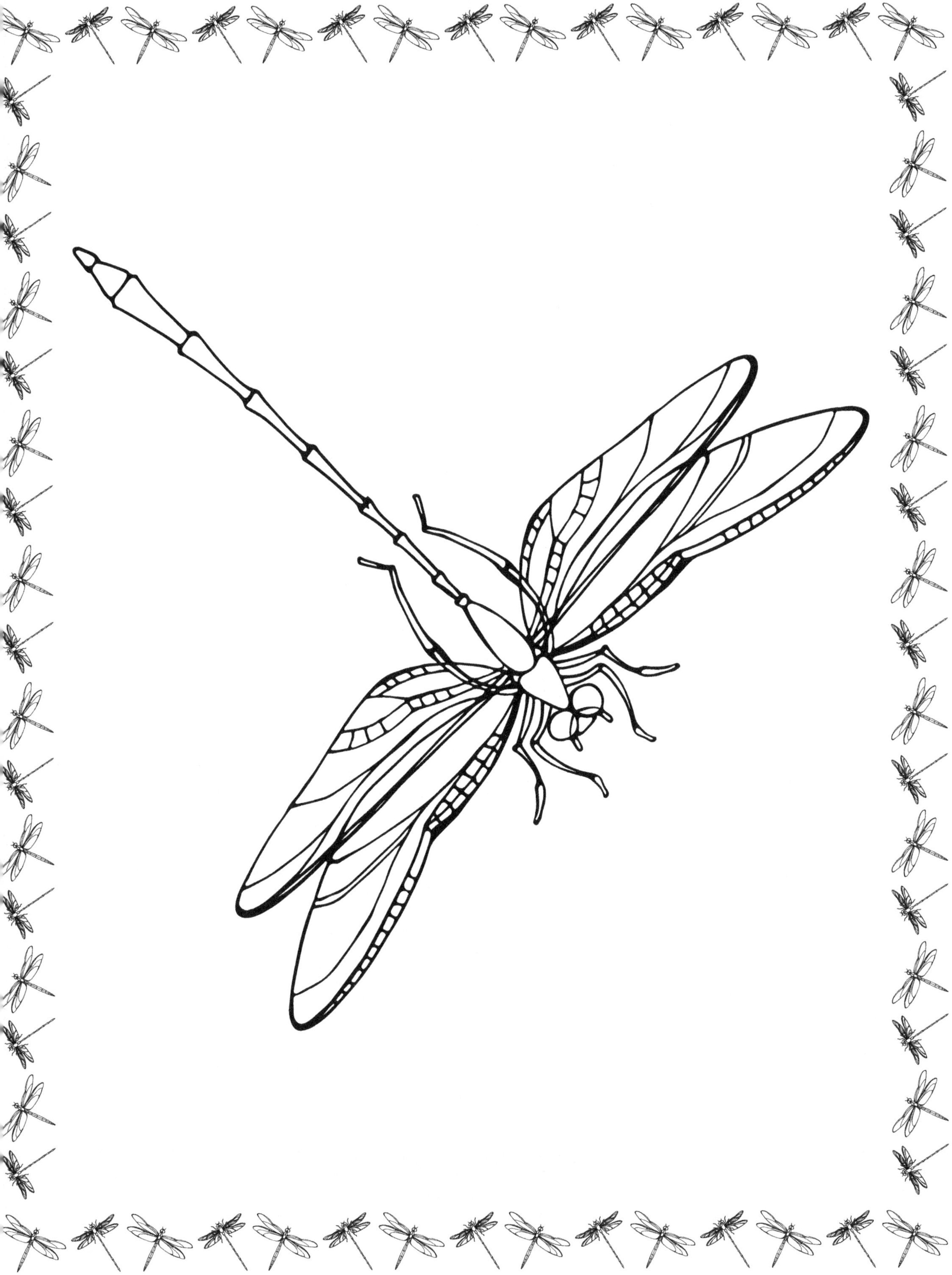

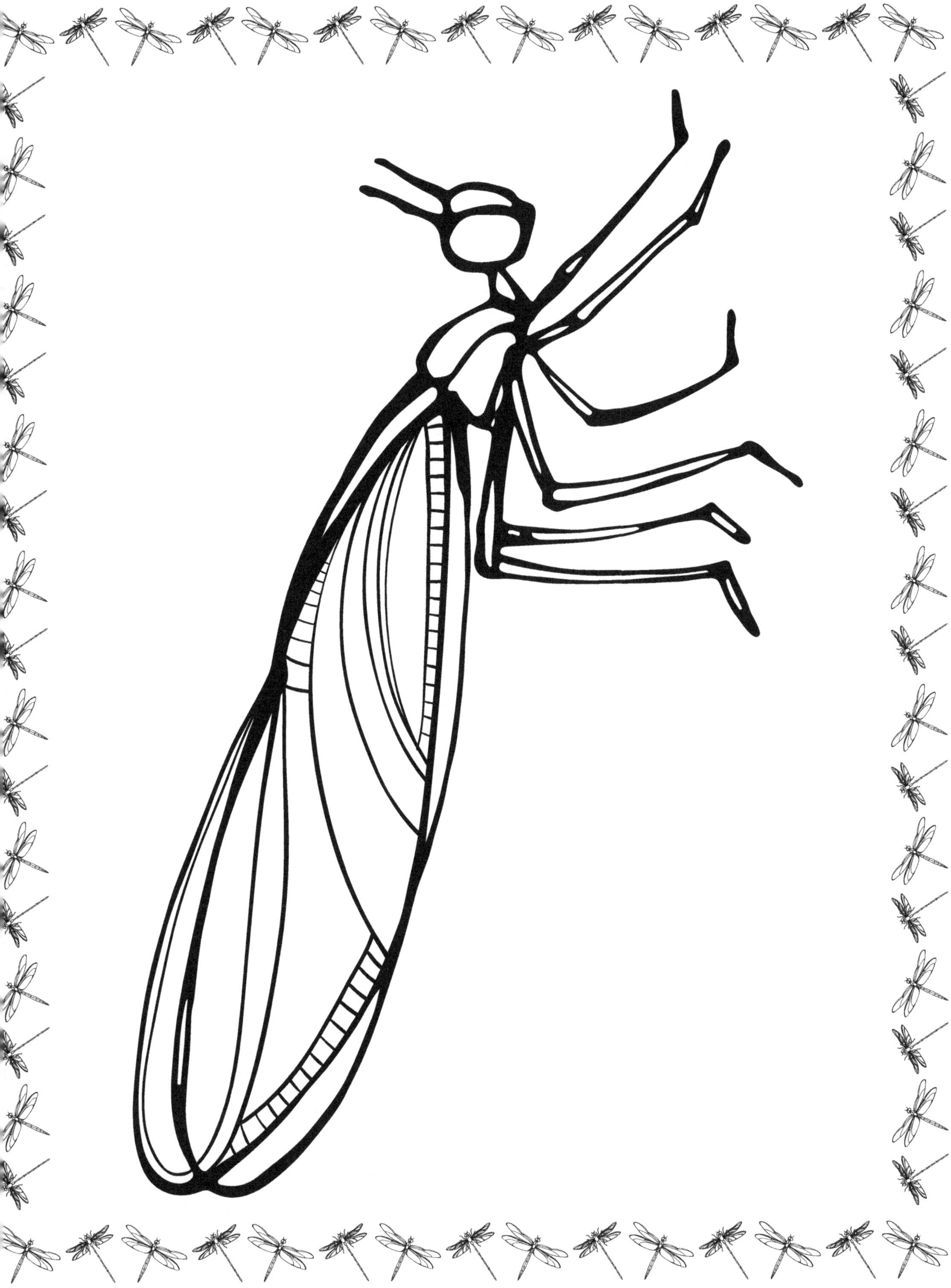

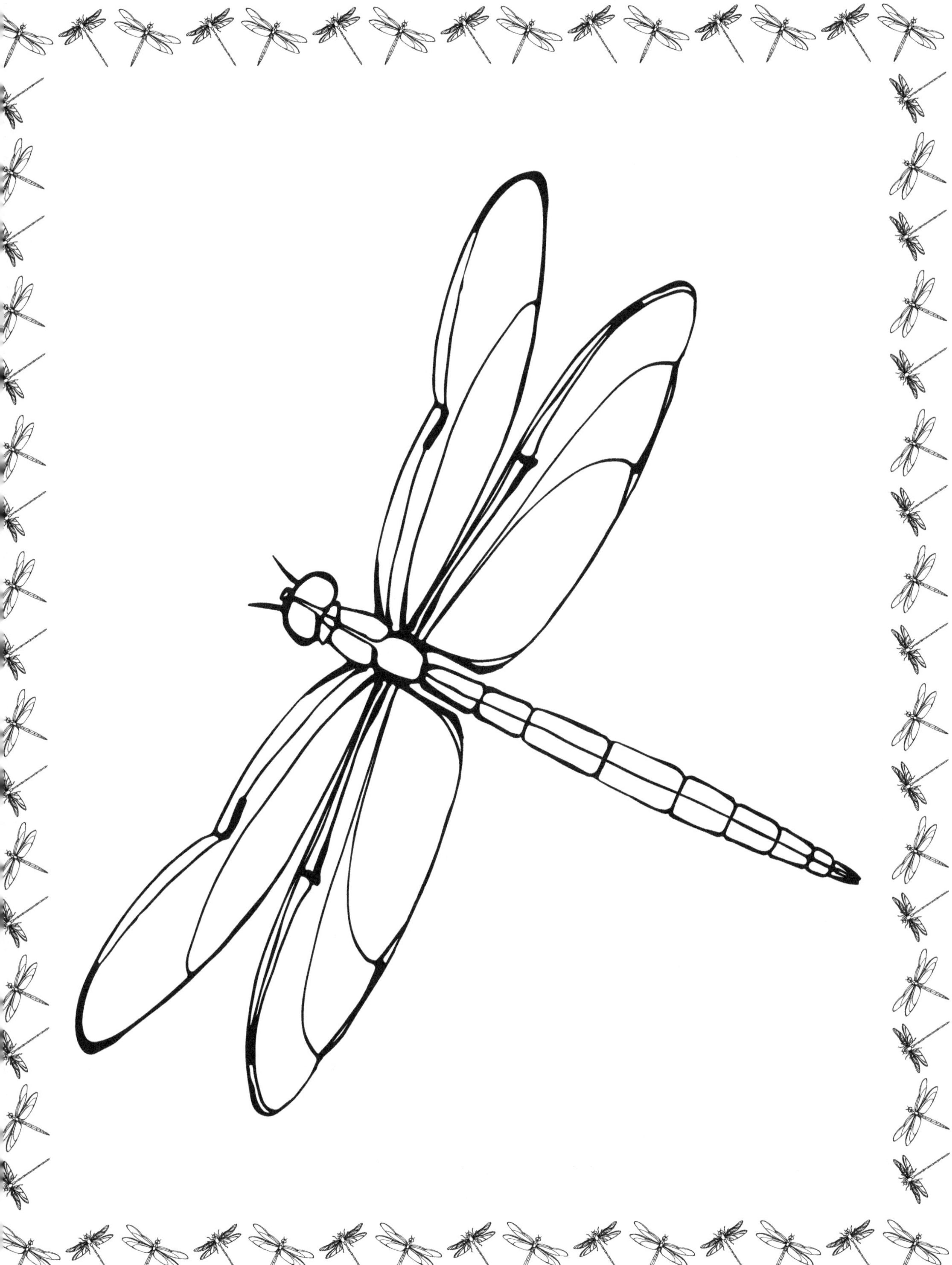

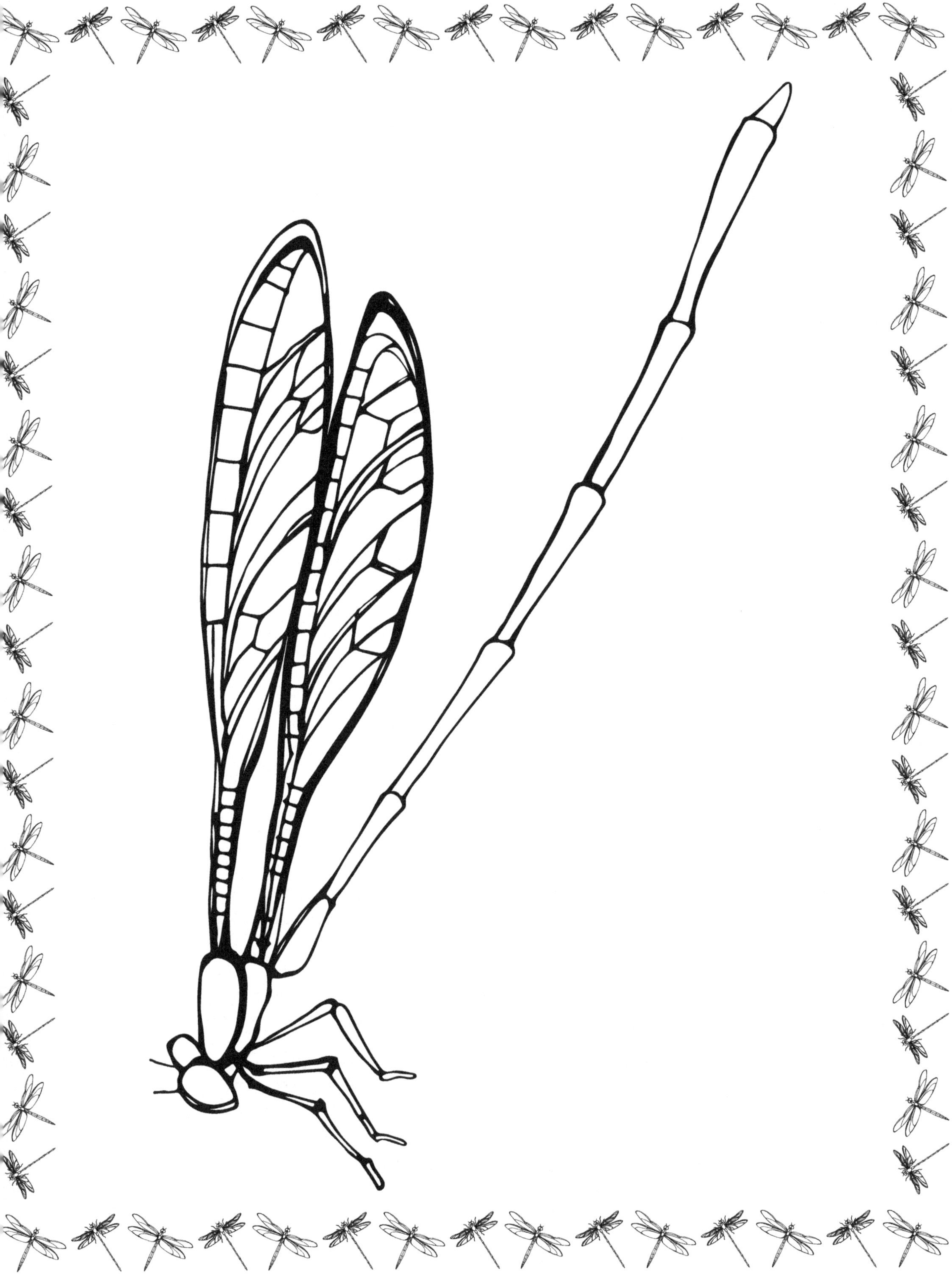

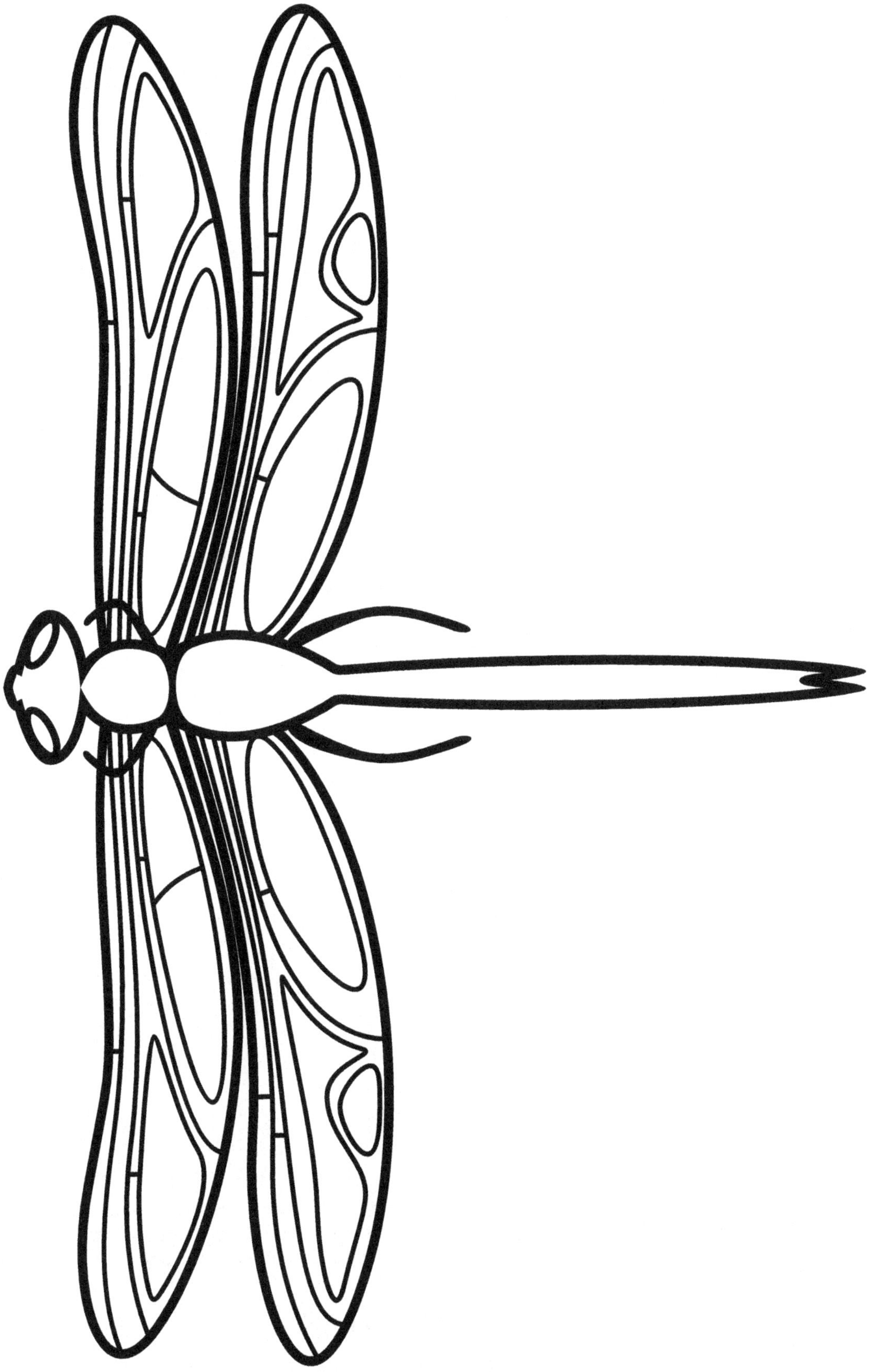

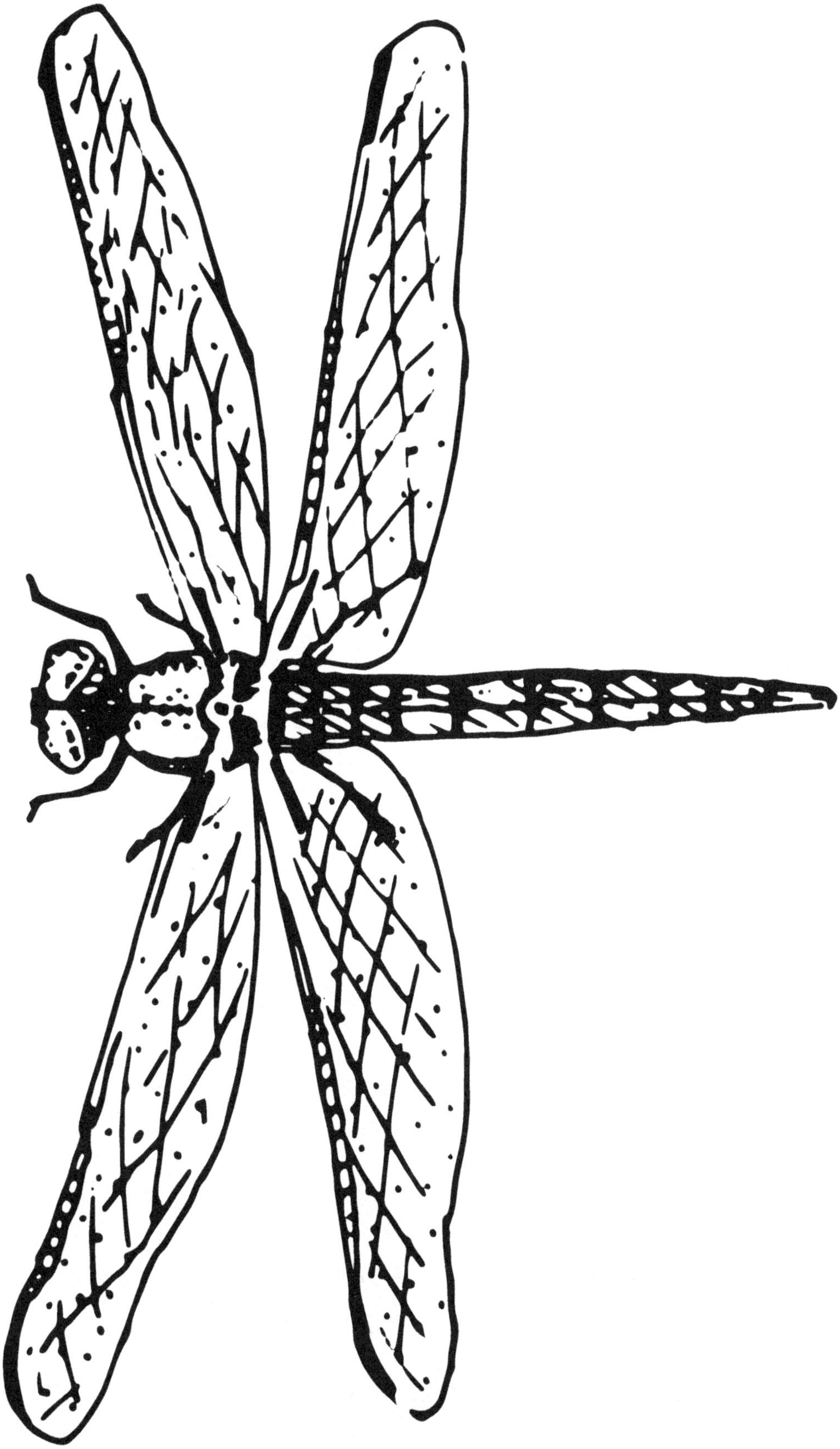

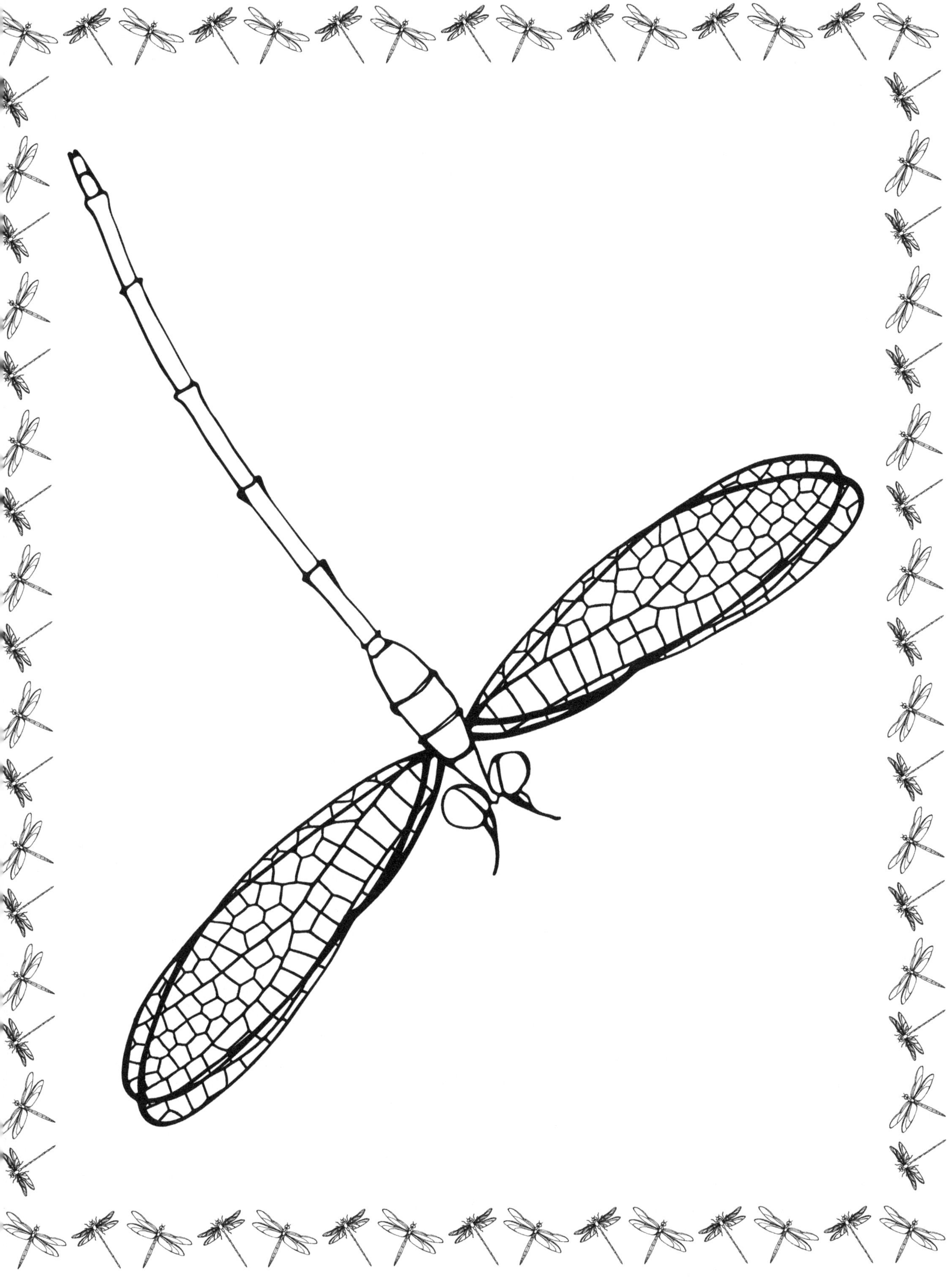

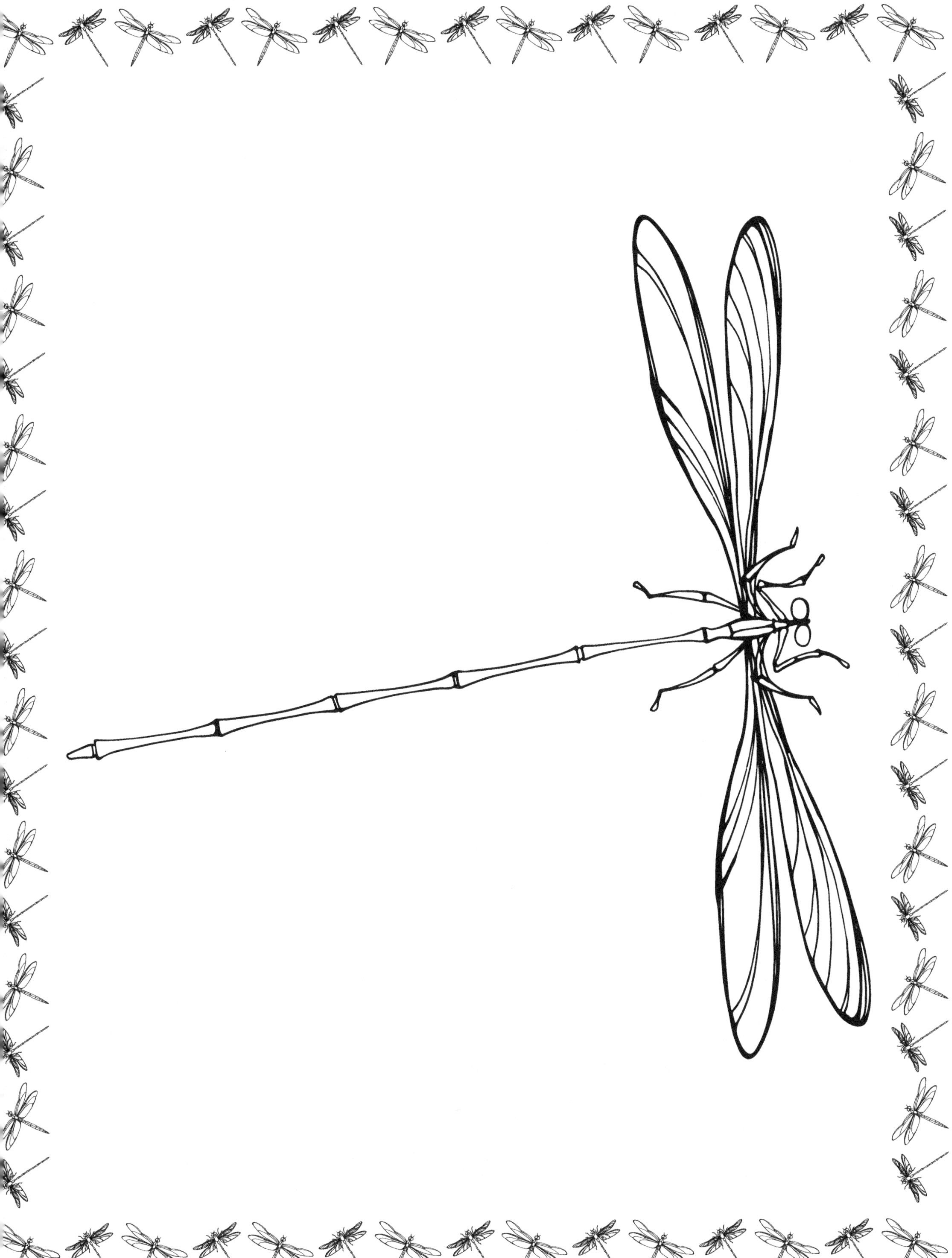

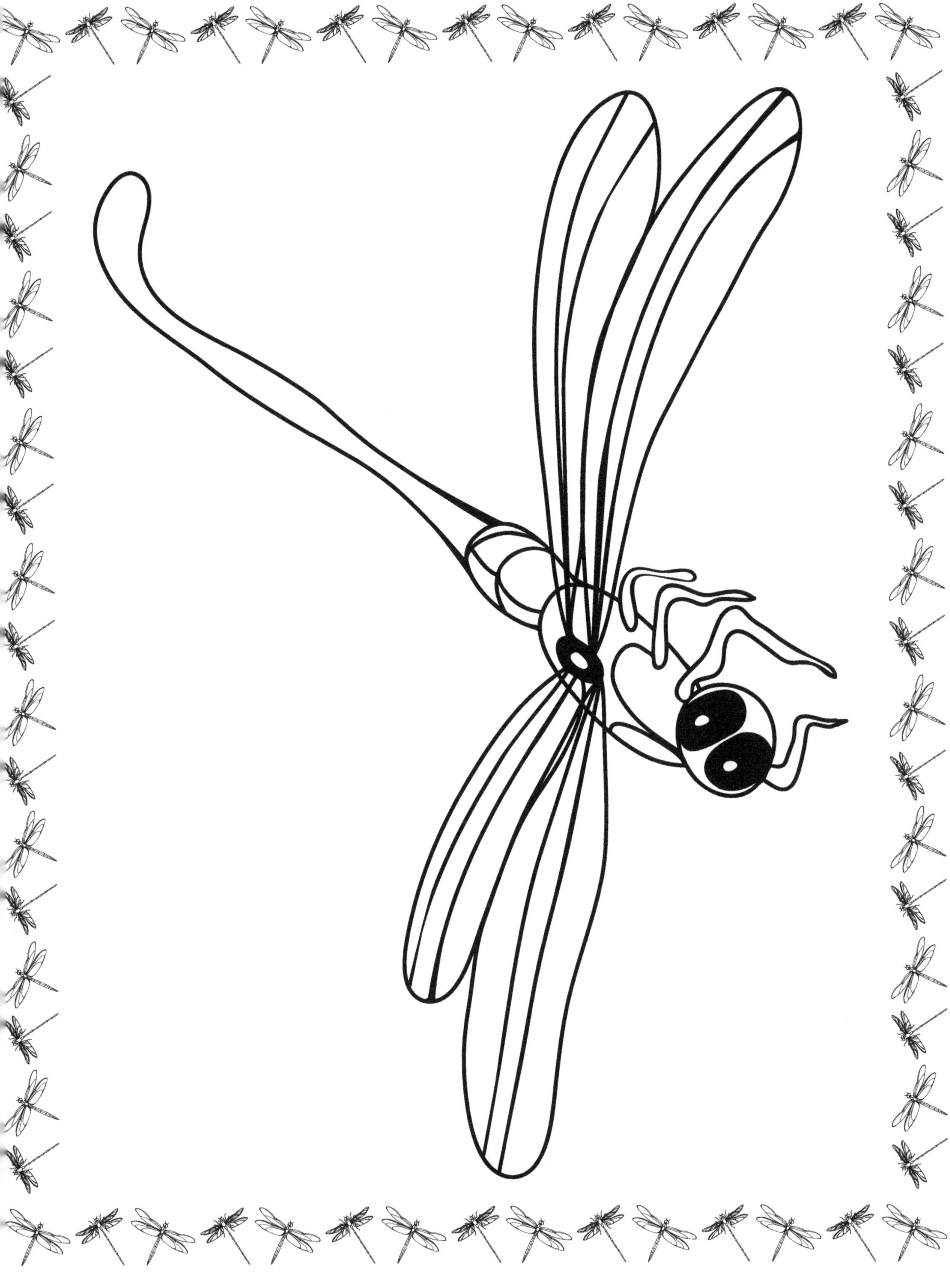

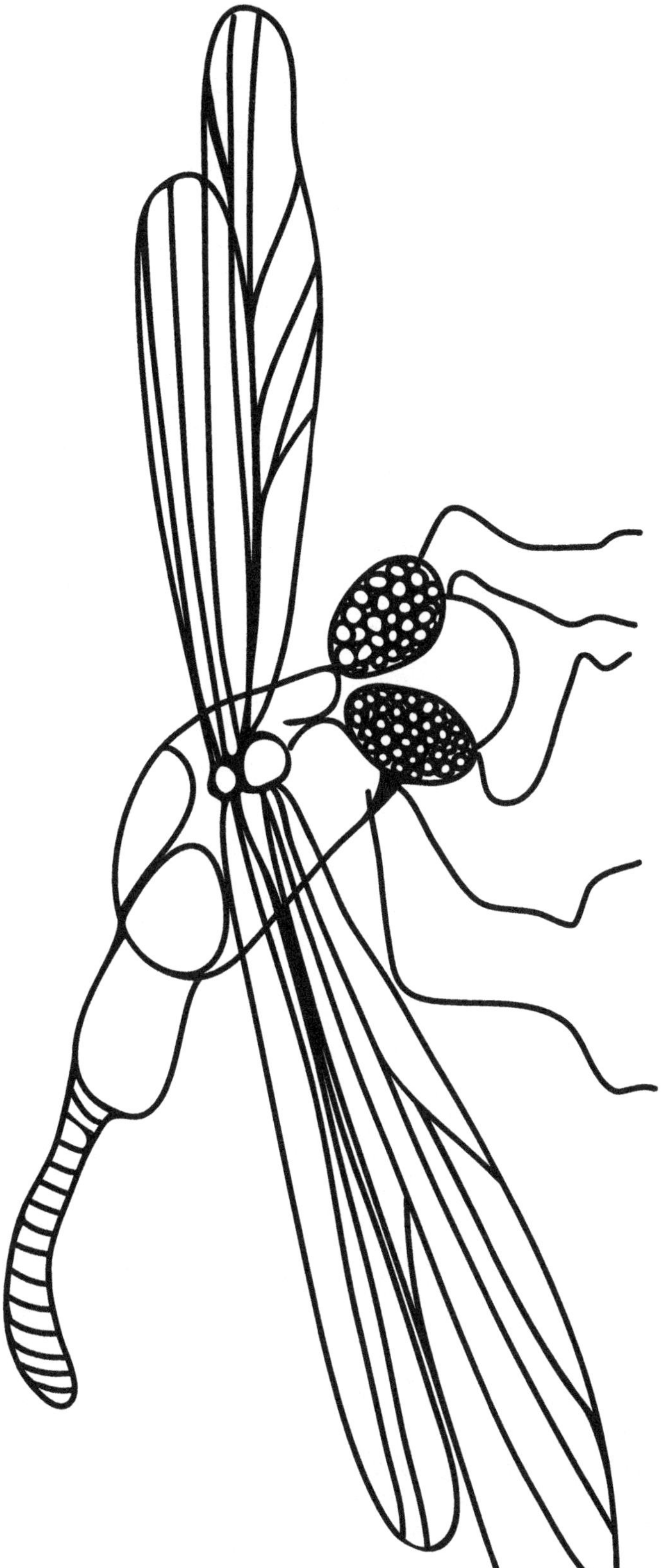

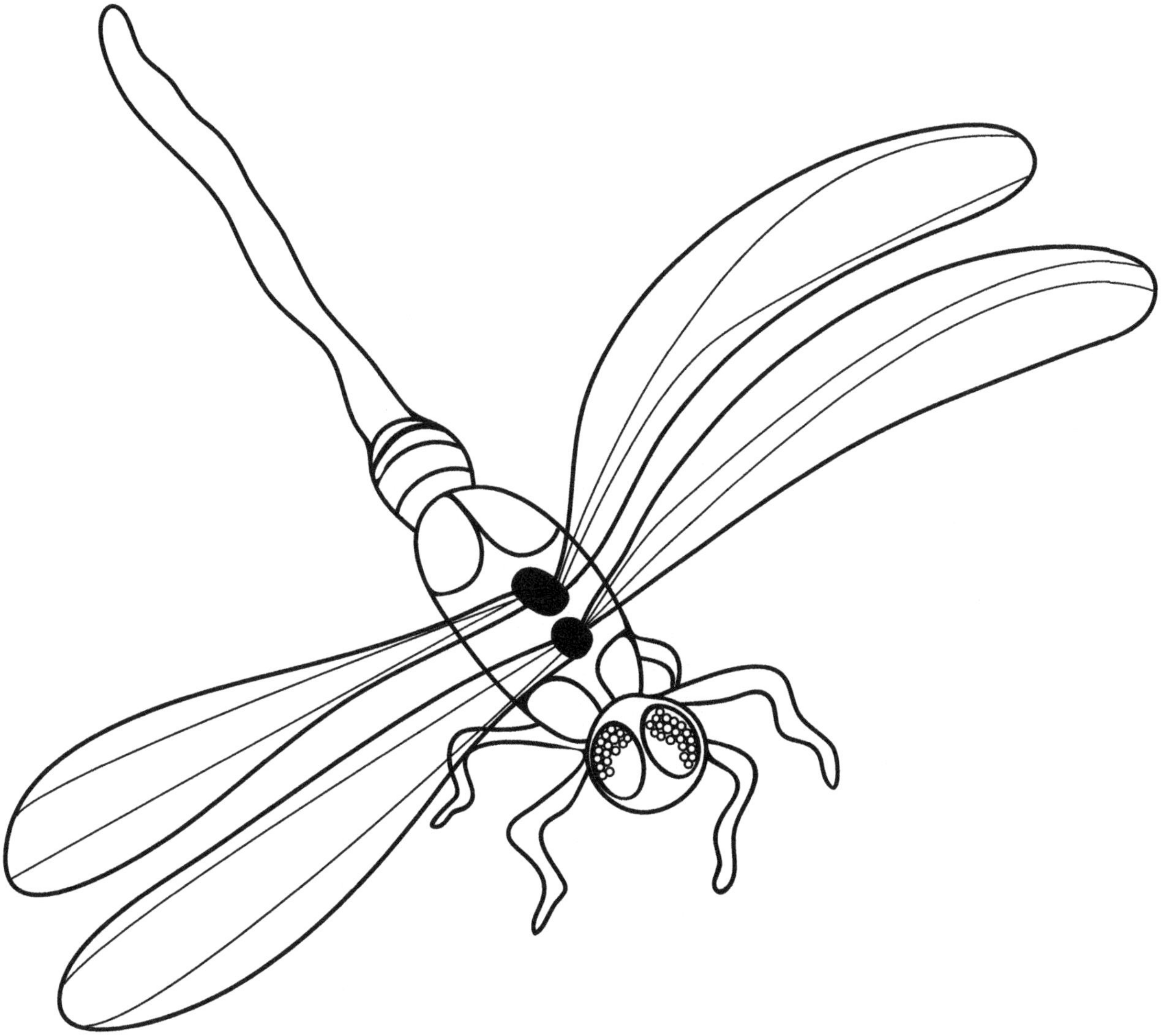

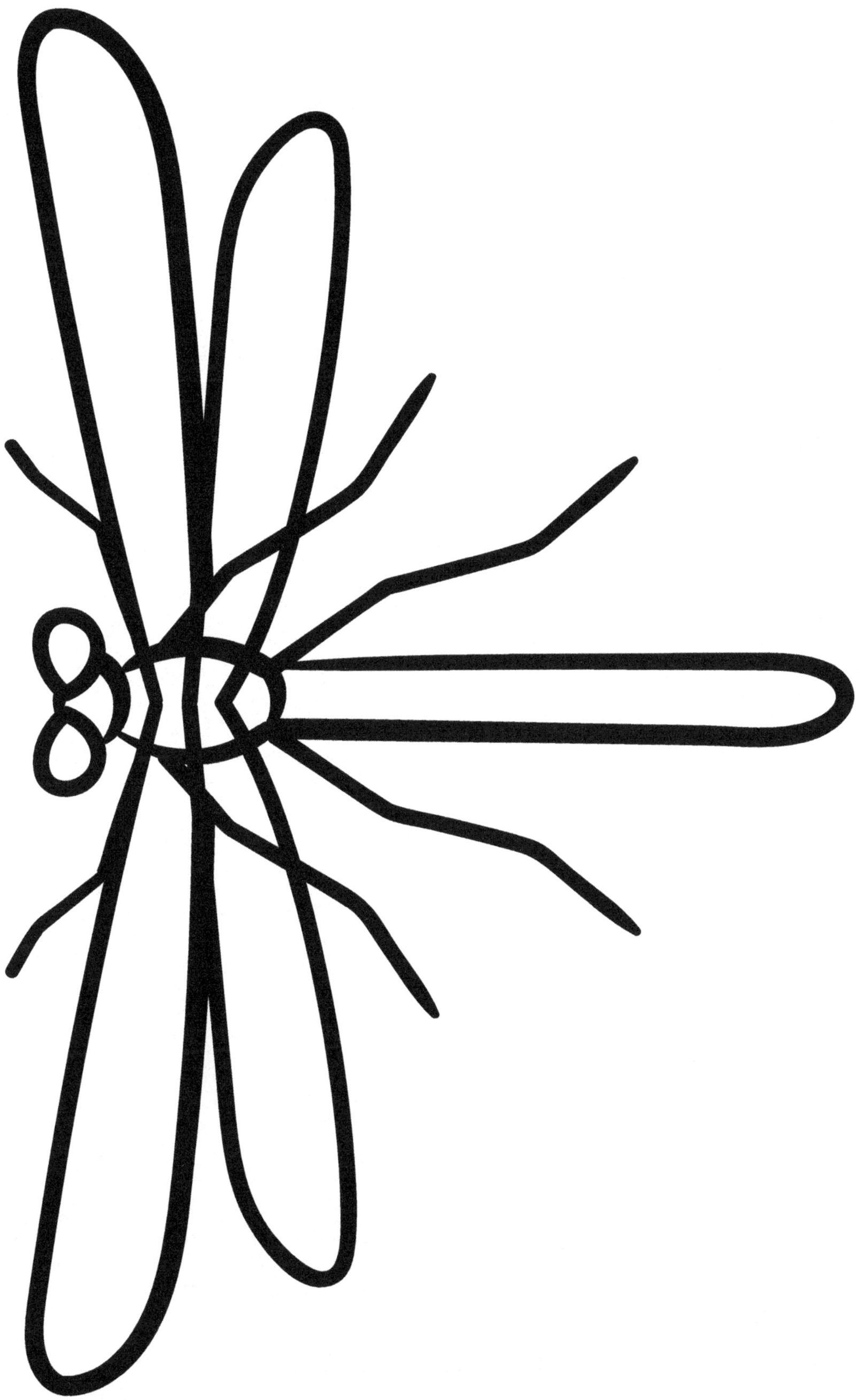

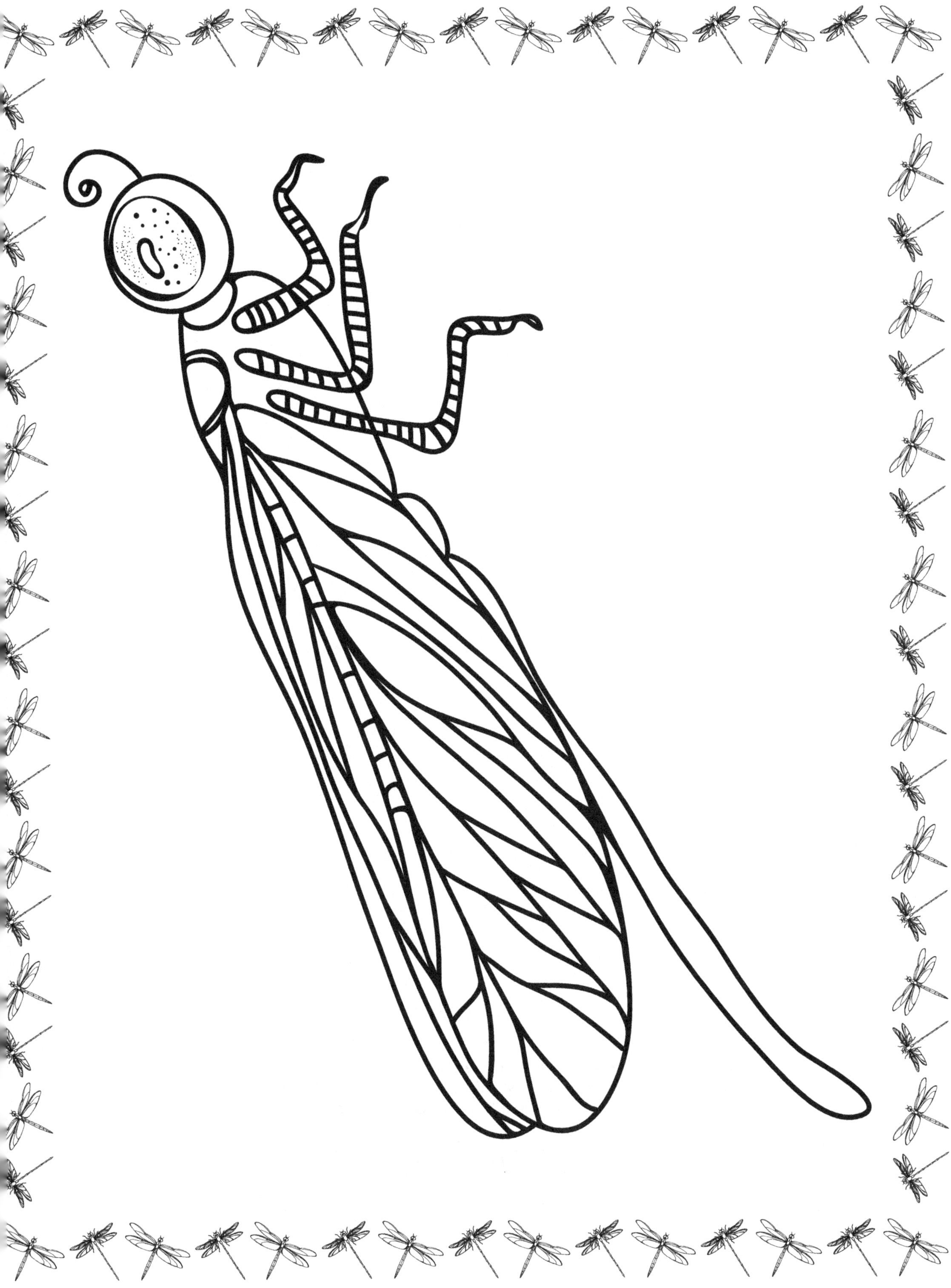

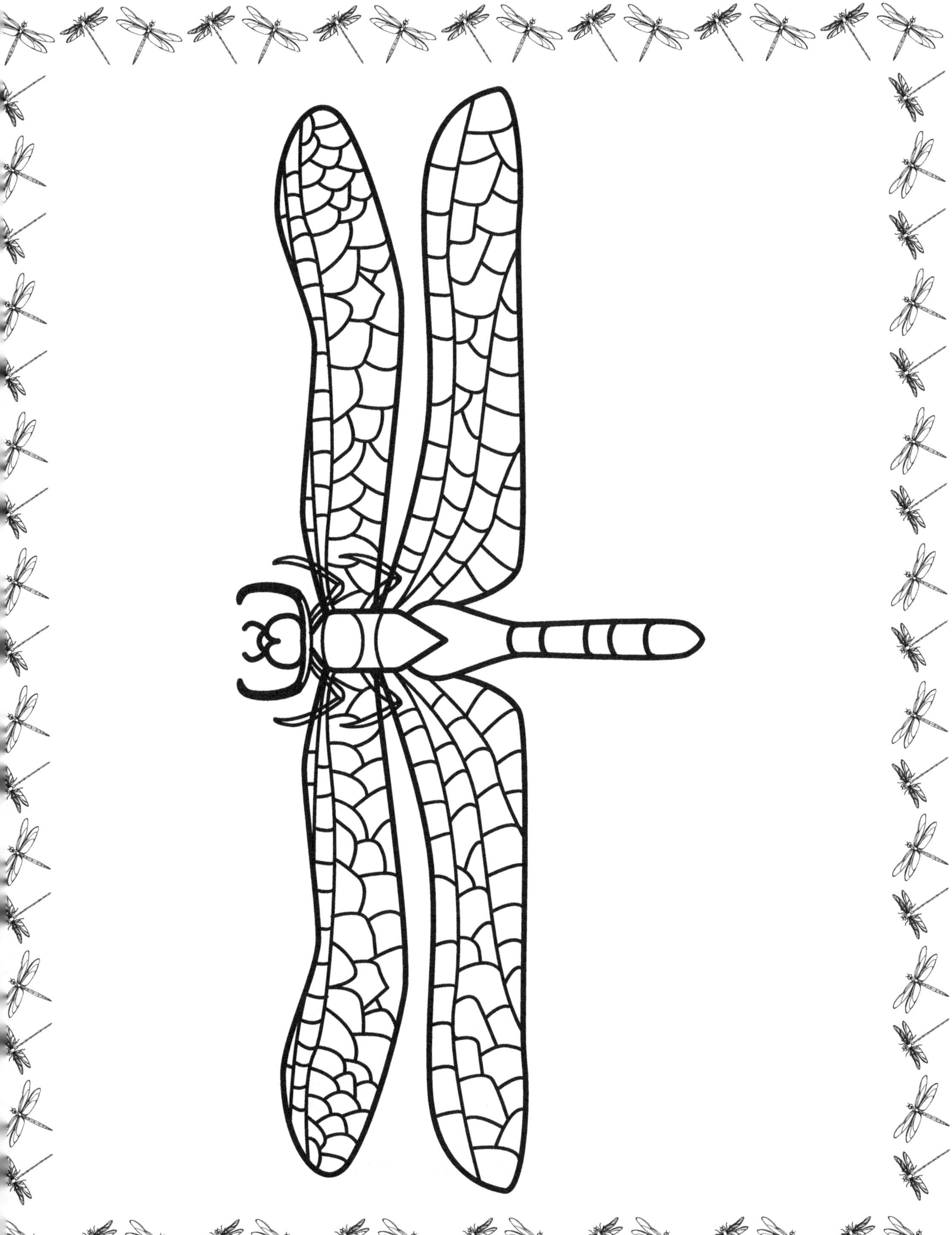

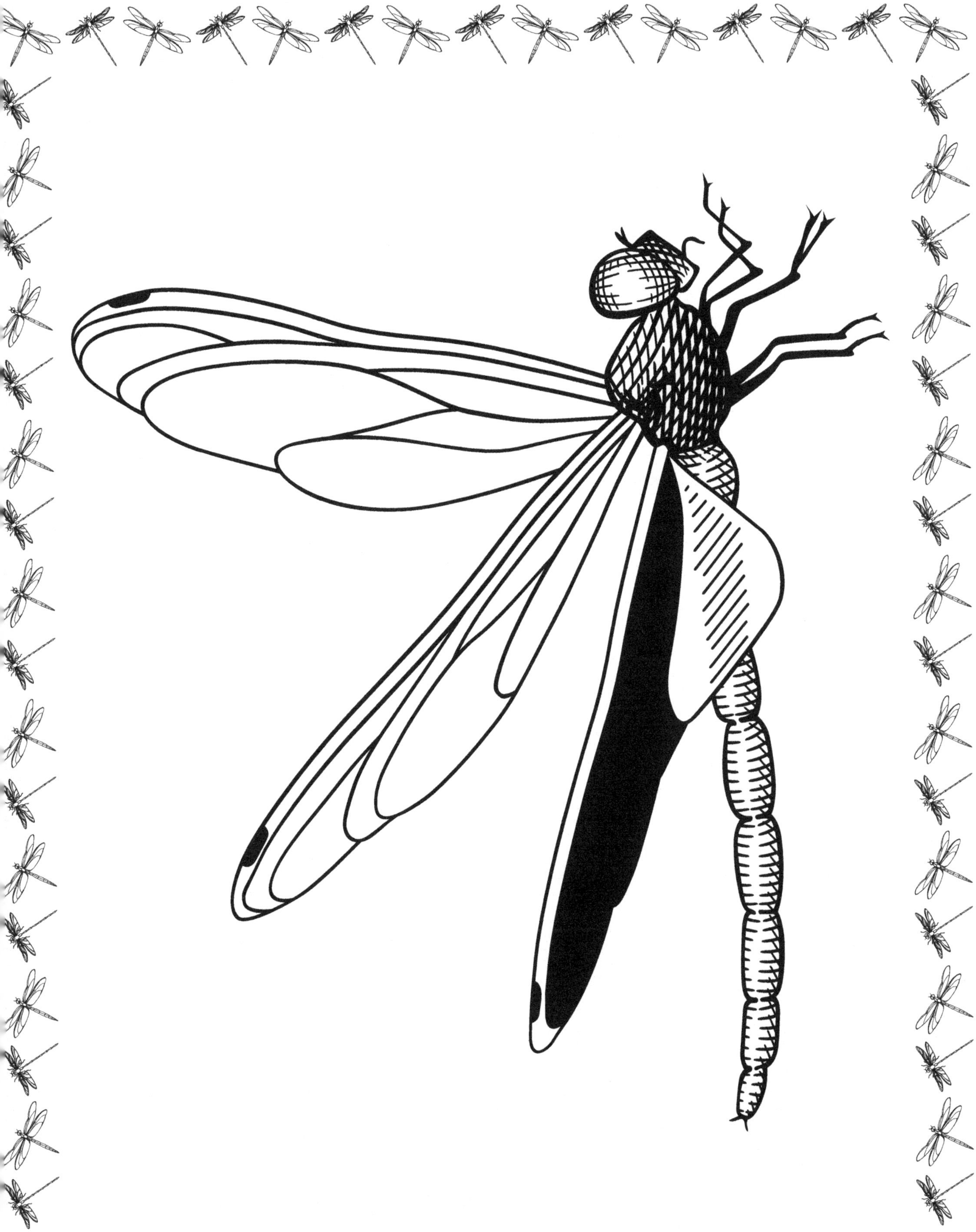

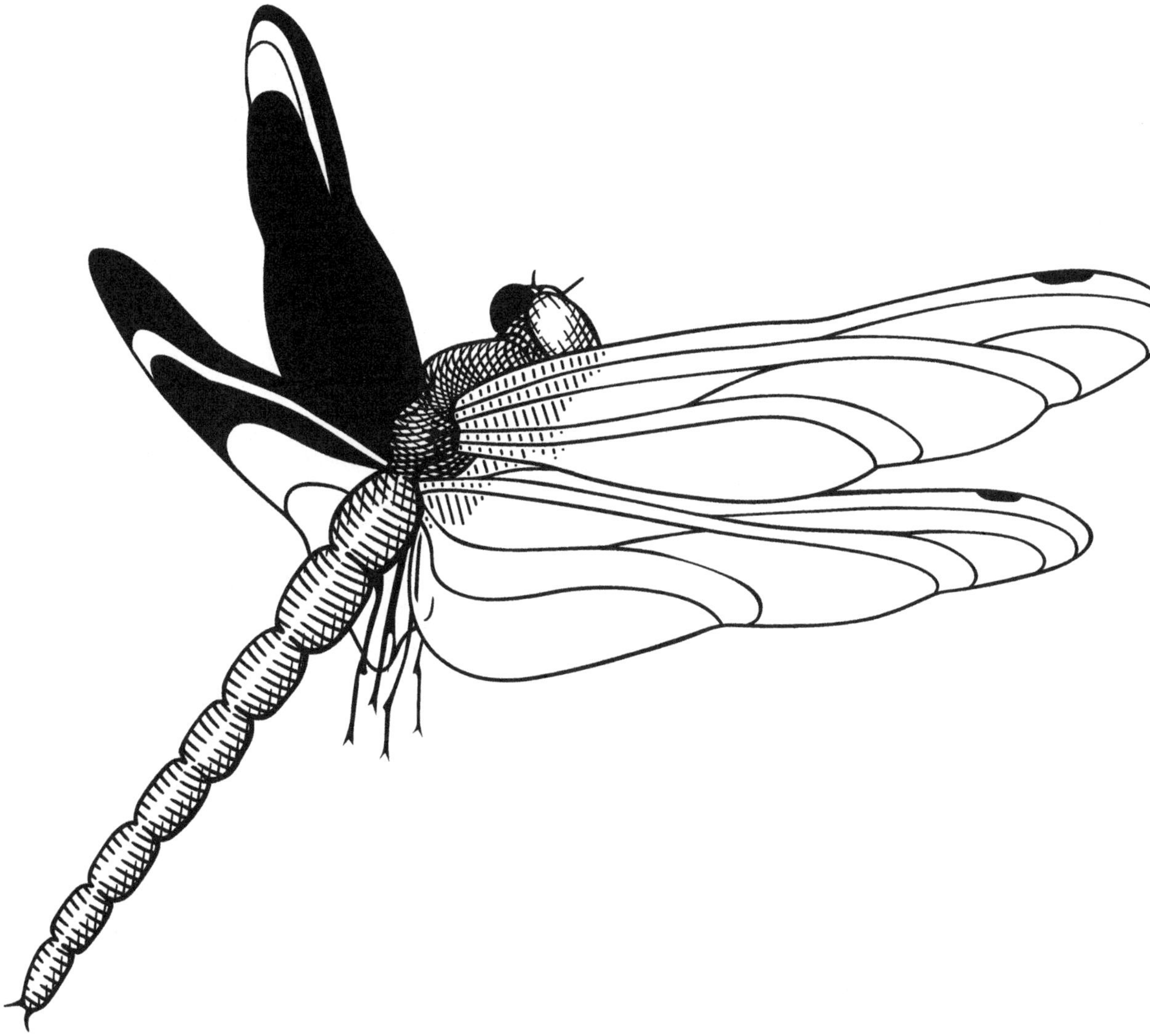

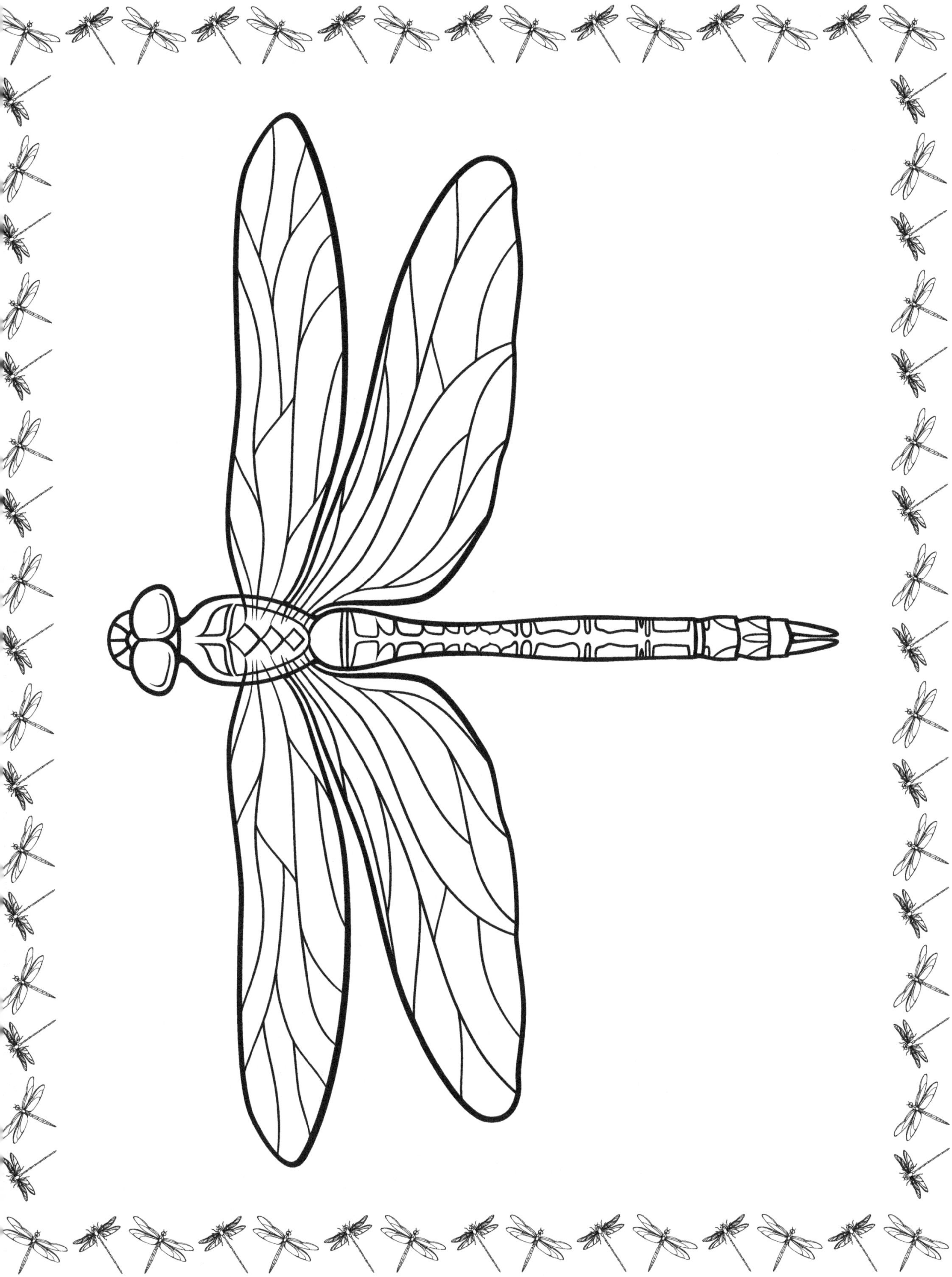

Made in the USA
Monee, IL
30 October 2020

46397197R00044